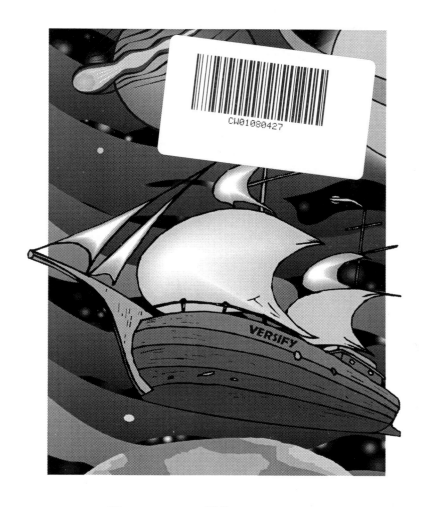

CW01080427

POETIC VOYAGES
TYNE & WEAR

Edited by Steve Twelvetree

First published in Great Britain in 2001 by
YOUNG WRITERS
Remus House,
Coltsfoot Drive,
Peterborough, PE2 9JX
Telephone (01733) 890066

HB ISBN 0 75433 394 9
SB ISBN 0 75433 395 7

FOREWORD

Young Writers was established in 1991 with the aim to promote creative writing in children, to make reading and writing poetry fun.

This year once again, proved to be a tremendous success with over 88,000 entries received nationwide.

The Poetic Voyages competition has shown us the high standard of work and effort that children are capable of today. It is a reflection of the teaching skills in schools, the enthusiasm and creativity they have injected into their pupils shines clearly within this anthology.

The task of selecting poems was therefore a difficult one but nevertheless, an enjoyable experience. We hope you are as pleased with the final selection in *Poetic Voyages Tyne & Wear* as we are.

CONTENTS

Lucy Marshall	36
Max Brown	36
Samantha Spencer	36
Laura Winder	37
Luke Garbutt	37
Craig Johnson	37
Mark Clapp	38
Zoë Bulch	38
Jessica Tonge	39
Joe Albert	39

Glebe Village Primary School

Steven Hodgson	40
David Wilson	40
Julie Bell	41
Kirsty English	41
Amy Hoogewerf	42
Andrew Green	42
Sam Witherspoon	43
Jamie McIntyre	43
Christopher McGrath	43
Carl Lockey	44

Grange Park Primary School

Courtney Wright	44
Rebecca Barnes	45
Graeme Loughlin	46
Marc Jenkinson	46
Adam Hepple	47
Taylor Davies	48
Ashley Burlinson	48
Jonathan Peverley	49
Bobby Ewart	50
Nathan Conlin	50
Jessica Richardson	51
Nicolle Braddick	52
James Cowie	52
Liam Anderson	53

St Mary's RC Primary School, Sunderland

Jessica Meldrum	73
Michael Quinn	74
Jessica Scarlett	74
Lydia Samy	75
Alex Shanks	76
Hannah Watson	76
Jenny Adshead	77
Anna Maltby	78
Connor Hall	78
Alice Wilson	79
Liam Gillespie	79
Hannah Mitchinson	80
Ben Herring	80
Lewis Monte	81
Martha Craggs	82
Anna White	82
Jack Bengochea	83
Adam McDade	83
Alice Haley	84
Joseph Collins	85
Zara Taylor	86
Leanne Hutcheon	86
Claudia Anderson	87
Sarah Anderson	87
Jonathan Meldrum	88
Clare Dewhurst	88
Jonathan Rasmussen	89
Jimmy Kordbarlag	89
Gabrielle O'Connnor	90
Daniel Dale	90
John-Paul Cosgrove	91
Jennifer Brown	91
Michael Simpson	92
James Beaton	92
Victoria Barlow	93
Victoria Campbell	94
Megan Campbell	95

Hannah Matterson	96
Meghan Turnbull	96
Bethany Patience	97
Hannah Jervis	98
Samantha Yewdell	98
Josh Parkinson	99
Michael Knox	99
Alexandra Cain	100

Stanhope County Primary School

Natalie Stidolph	100
Louise Young	101
Ashleigh Keenan	102
Kassie Waugh	102
Victoria Liscombe	103
Emmy Simpson	103
James McElwee	104
Jonathan Wilson	104
Paul Nygaard	105
Anthony Hall	105
Lyndsey McGowell	106
Kayleigh Kirkley	106
Lauren Caizley	107
Dean Bill	107
Melissa Liddle	107
Robyn Hamilton	108
Michael Lister	108
Leonard Oxley	109
Lee Alderson	109
Lewis McHaffie	109
Victoria Naisby	110
Rachel Codling	110
Michael Smith	111
Jessica Lee	111
Andrea Gilmour	112
Liam Fraser	112
Adam Ratcliffe	113

Witherwack Primary School

The Poems

A TRIP TO THE MOON

I felt like going to the moon,
So I flew up on a balloon,
Then I saw I was very high,
By now I was way up in the sky.
I looked around it seemed like space,
Then I saw the moon and it looked like a face.
I looked around and I saw some stars,
Then I noticed they were right next to Mars.
The balloon burst,
And I fell head first.
I crashed home with a big boom,
Then I was back home in my room.

Chloe Williamson (9)
Ashley Primary School

SPACE

When I got to space
I took one pace
And walked over the floor
And broke the ship door.

I saw an alien and ran and ran
And whacked it with a pan
I saw all the stars
I went to Mars
I went to the moon
I left it so soon.

Fraser James Carlson (8)
Ashley Primary School

DESERT ISLAND

Sailing the seven seas
As I see an island with coconut palm trees.
Then suddenly came a storm and an April shower
It rained and rained with all its power,
I was trying and trying to grip hard to the ship,
It wasn't easy I had to admit.
The wind was in my eyes and I couldn't see where I was going.
The ship was going to crash
The rough current was flowing.
The ship went to the bottom of the sea.
The only survivor was me.
I swam to the island ahead
I made a little shelter,
And went to bed.

Francesca Martin (8)
Ashley Primary School

JOURNEY OF A LIFETIME

High in the air the spaceship flew
Over the sky into the blue.

Flying over across the sky
The spaceship feels like it's going to die.

Jumping, leaping over the stars
Over the planets right over Mars.

Karim El-Shakankery (9)
Ashley Primary School

FOUNTAIN SHOOT

I was swimming along
In the Mediterranean sea
Soon I was on a wet grey thing
'What's happening to me'
There was a funny noise
And the whip of a tail
I was lifted up high in the air
'Oh my gosh I am on a whale'
Suddenly I am lifted higher
With a spray of water
I am chucked on to the shore
There is Mrs Porter
She helped me clear off the foam
Then I woke up in my bed back home.

Natalie Burrough (8)
Ashley Primary School

A TRIP TO MARS

I dreamed I went to Mars
And counted the stars.
They were very bright
It was a great night.

I saw a rocket
And looked in my pocket.
I found some space money
When I woke up I thought it was funny.

Michelle Smith (8)
Ashley Primary School

FUTURAMA

I started off in my spaceship
Of the handles I got a good grip
I landed with a bump
And the ground felt like a big, huge flump.

Three green aliens came along
They started singing a song
They got out their limbo stick
And started giving their noses a pick.

They started to fight me
It was one on to three
They were in the middle of a scheme
Suddenly I woke up and it had all been a dream.

Sophie Dodds (8)
Ashley Primary School

THE ARMY

When I join the army I'll get into my tank
And the enemy ships will be sunk.
I'll throw up the grenade
And start the air raid
When I'm in a plane,
I'll go positively insane.
When I'm in a sub
I'd rather be at the pub.

David Lawrenson (10)
Ashley Primary School

TRAGIC IN SPACE

5, 4, 3, 2, 1 off we go,
Going to a planet that we do not know.
Jason and Marc controlled the rocket,
I looked at the door, I remembered
I forgot to lock it.

The door swung open and I got sucked out,
I looked around and I started to shout.
While I was up in the air,
I looked down and there was nothing there.

They threw out a rope and pulled me back in,
Jason looked at me and gave me a grin.
We did not see the planet but we got to the Moon,
Bing! Bang! Boom! I was in my room.

Sherri Robinson (9)
Ashley Primary School

ROCKET UP TO SPACE

I went up to space in my rocket
I landed up on Mars
I saw a lot of planets
And a lot of stars
I went across to Jupiter
Then across to the Moon
I did not know how long I had been
Time went so soon.

David Geach (9)
Ashley Primary School

ANIMALS WE LIKE

My mam likes dolphins,
My dad likes pigs,
My sister likes animals that are nice and big.
My nanna likes dogs,
And I like cats,
My grandad likes little black bats.

My uncle likes fish,
My auntie likes bears,
My cousin likes big fast hares.
More and more which are alike,
These are the animals my family like.

Nicole Williams (10)
Ashley Primary School

THE VOYAGE THROUGH SPACE

As a meteorite shower flies through the black sky,
Our spaceship flies with it, the crew in and I.
Dashing quicker, quicker and faster by the hour,
Everybody thinking that we might run out of power.

One other spacecraft trapped on planet Mars
That's where we are going after whizzing through these stars.
We will try to get to them as their lives are at stake,
We really want to save them.
We hope it's not too late.

Victoria Addison (8)
Ashley Primary School

SHILOH

I have a friend called Shiloh
When we play we have a laugh.
She likes to play outside
Where she gets dirty but she doesn't like to bath.

Her hair is black and shiny
It sparkles in the sun.
She never has to brush or comb it,
Even when we've had some fun.

She does not bath or wash or comb
She lives with us in our home.
She's not a fish or a cat or a frog,
She's my best friend, she's my dog.

Jennie Dinning (10)
Ashley Primary School

MAD ABOUT DOGS

Dogs are nice, dogs are rough
I like dogs so very much
Mongrels, poodles, bulldogs too,
I do like dogs so very much.

Dogs are fluffy, cuddly too
I do like dogs so very much
I do, I do, I do
Do you?

Michaela Surtees (10)
Ashley Primary School

A Journey To Outer Space

Looking at the stars
including Pluto and Mars,
going up in space,
is like winning the human race.
I like space,
It's not a disgrace.

Landing on Mars
eating Milky Way bars,
jumping over the moon,
landing in a space swimming pool.
I like space,
It's not a disgrace.

Sitting in a rocket,
eating space lockets,
landing on the sun,
it's boiling hot for me to run.
I like space,
It's not a disgrace.

Gary Wilkin (10)
Ashley Primary School

The Human Race And Aliens

Aliens are coming
How stunning.
They're coming for the human race
Wow look at that alien's face.
They're here
Oh! the fear
The tension is killing me!
It's thrilling me!

It's starting . . . go!
And they're off!
The aliens boo
The humans cheer while they drink beer
Number one breaks down, number four wins
They all cheer for number four.

Scott Bullock (9)
Ashley Primary School

FUTURE

Going to that working place
Just beginning the human race.
What's it like at the senior school,
Is it class or funky or cool?

Or is it like a mouldy pear
Going brown with extra hair?
Will I have to work so hard
That I sweat and smell like lard?

After I've finished all of that,
I'll probably be starting to get fat.
Soon, by now, I'll be learning to drive
It'll be easier than trying to dive.
A car will cost lots of cash,
Will the metal grind and smash?

Probably now I'll have a job,
Working in a lousy shop,
Or will it be funky and cool
Like that scary senior school?

Charlie McCann (9)
Ashley Primary School

THE DREAM

I lie in my bed
With thoughts in my head.
I'm going to the moon
I'll be there very soon.
I fly in the sky
Oh my it's very high.
I fly past the stars
And get a glimpse of Mars.
I see the moon
I'll be there very soon.

Amy Craig (8)
Ashley Primary School

DRIVING

Driving down the lane,
Brum, brum we go
Crashing! Into a wheely bin,
Crash, crash, oh no!

Bouncing up and down
Up and down the lane
I'm driving carefully
No! I'm driving insane!

Jill Quantrill (10)
Ashley Primary School

AUTUMN

Autumn can be fun
Especially when out comes the sun.
Cobwebs glistening in the night
Leaves shine in the moonlight.

In autumn, trees shed their leaves
They come fluttering down in the gentle breeze.
Brightly coloured leaves blow round
Leaves brown, red, yellow, lie on the ground.

Squirrels collecting nuts to eat
Crinkled leaves under my feet.
Hedgehogs eating lots of snails
Leaves blowing in the gales.

Sophie Falloon (9)
Donwell Primary School

BONFIRE NIGHT!

It's the 5th of November,
So read this and remember.

Tonight is the night they go off,
The smoke makes you cough.

The fireworks fly,
And sparkle in my eye.

Bonfire Night, Bonfire Night,
They are wonderful and bright.

Emma Greener (8)
Donwell Primary School

MEMORIES

When I was a little girl
I went to Edinburgh Zoo.
There were lots of different animals
Tigers, lions too.

Big scary reptiles and lizards with sick slivery tongues
Spitting and lashing that's what they like to do.

It was feeding time and all the kids jumped with joy
As the penguins waddled down the path
To find their loot of all.
All the birds flapped their wings
As the food was thrown to them.

What a joy and interest for us all
To visit Edinburgh Zoo.

Stephanie Gallon (9)
Donwell Primary School

CHRISTMAS POEM

C is for the Christmas lights on the tree
H is for the holly what hangs on the door.
R is for the wrapping paper on the toys.
I is for the icicles hanging on the rooftops.
S is for Santa coming down the chimney.
T is for toys for all the boys and girls.
M is for mistletoe where people kiss.
A round the Christmas tree there's presents.
S is for the tinsel that sparkles on the tree.

Christopher Johnson (11)
Donwell Primary School

SPORT

Cricket is fantastic,
Cricket is good,
Some people watch it,
Like everyone should.

Football's played by boys
Girls play it too.
Who always wins the Premiership?
It's Man U!

Tennis is fast,
And played over a net.
Tim Henman will always win,
I will bet.

Rugby is quite dangerous,
You have to be tough.
Ouch! Ouch! Ouch! Ouch!
It's very, very rough.

Stephen Maughan (10)
Donwell Primary School

CHRISTMAS POEM

Robins with red bellies
Mothers making raspberry jelly,
The Christmas dinner is smelly,
Soon we're gonna have fat bellies.
All the presents under the tree,
Santa's been on a shopping spree!

Sophie Nesbitt (8)
Donwell Primary School

SAD JAMIE

There was a boy called Jamie,
Who had a cousin called Amy,
He was not allowed to see his Dad,
Which made him very, very sad.

He could always talk to his friend,
Who sometimes gave him things to lend,
He talked to his teacher,
Who acted like a strange creature!

One day he went to school,
Which was transformed into a pool,
He had a very cool car,
Which would drive pretty far.

I had a friend called Ken,
Who every week turned into a hen,
He was the best one I had,
But sometimes he was pretty mad!

Jamie Young (11)
Donwell Primary School

THERE WAS A YOUNG BOY CALLED SCOTT

There was a young boy called Scott
He liked to saw wood a lot.
He made a good plane
Flew off to Spain
That clever young boy called Scott.

Scott Matthews (10)
Donwell Primary School

IN THE BATHROOM

Have you ever wondered how strange the bathroom is?
All those little holes where the spiders live.
Have you ever pondered what occurs when you flush the loo?
And how the water just appears out of nowhere too?
Have you ever thought why your dad sings in the shower?
And when you peep your head around the curtain,
                              he explodes at you in full power!
So, my friends, let me give you some useful advice,
Never go in when your dad is in,
He's a dangerous device!

Melanie Sheehy (11)
Donwell Primary School

ROASTING RED

His mane is red,
Leaves are his bed,
He glistens in the sun,
While he sizzles like bacon in a bun.

He is the king of the jungle,
He doesn't get in a mumble,
He is not dim,
His roar is not like a hymn.

He sleeps through the dusk.
Do not surprise him and he will not hurt thus,
He hunts his prey,
And eats in May.

Matthew Freeburn (10)
Donwell Primary School

MY PETS

I have two cats,
One fat, one vicious.
They both eat their food,
And think it's delicious.
Trixy scratches, Colin catches,
Birds and mice -
He thinks they're nice,
They lie on my bed,
And lick my head,
But they don't sleep until they're fully fed.

I also have a fish,
Who lives in a dish.
Charlie's his name,
And the cats have a game.
Where they slip in their paws
Like big furry oars.
Charlie doesn't like that,
And thinks 'Go away cat.'

Trixy, Colin and Charlie too,
You're my pets, and I love you.

Hannah Weddle (8)
Donwell Primary School

WWF 2001

WWF is the best,
If you mess with Kane, you mess with death.
The Undertaker will make you drop,
From a 60 foot building when he pushes you off.
And that's the bottom line cos Stone Cold said so!

Nathan Dawson (10)
Donwell Primary School

VALENTINE'S DAY

V alentine's cards
A lot of chocolates from your admirer
L ots of love cards
E veryone is in love
N ice chocolate hearts
T hinking about your true love
I sn't he so cute.
N ever stop getting Valentine's cards
E ndless love
S ecret admirers.

D evoted boys
A lways loving them
Y ou'll never stop loving Valentine's Day.

Rachel Cockburn (10)
Donwell Primary School

MY RAT

My rat likes to play
If she could she'd play all day
She always does as she is told,
And she is really nice to hold.

She always plays up on the table,
And she will chew it if she's able.
But she will only leave it alone
If it is as hard as stone.

My rat.

Susan Gilbert (11)
Donwell Primary School

I AM NOT . . .

I'm not a rainbow in the sky,
I'm not a bird flying high,
I'm not a dog that barks so loud,
I'm not a soft, fluffy cloud,
I'm not a teacher that teaches art,
I'm not a kid that is so smart,
I'm not a doctor that cures,
I'm not a rat in the sewers,
I'm not a book writer,
I'm not a librarian that types on the typer,
I'm not a school head,
I'm not the least bit dead,
I'm not a fish in the sea,
But thank you Lord for making me!

Danielle Huddleston (11)
Donwell Primary School

NIGHTMARE

Swish, swash,
All night through.
Why can't I sleep but how can you?
I dreamt I was alone, alone, alone,
And strangled by my Auntie's phone.
Then the door made a loud bang,
Then whispers I heard as spirits sang.

Katherine Madden (11)
Donwell Primary School

JANE

A little girl called Jane,
Smashed a windowpane.
She couldn't pay for the glass,
So she asked her very small class,
But they refused and pushed her down the lane.

The cost was way too much,
Money was something she couldn't touch.
So she robbed a bank,
But the money sank
On the way home to Dutch.

Louise Taylor (10)
Donwell Primary School

ARMY

One day I signed up for the army
Me mam said I was barmy
The army said they're going to decide,
I went to my house in the meantime
I drank my last mango and lime.

The time had come,
They said I have to sign a form and it's done.
They told me to get in a plane,
It was pouring with rain.
I was wearing goggles, I looked like a clown,
Then I got shot down.

Jonathan Herron Evans (10)
Donwell Primary School

COLD WINTER

Snow dropping off the trees,
Children playing on the ice,
Snowman getting built.

Walking to school,
Hands are frozen,
Snow is soft,
Snow is white.

People wearing gloves,
People wearing hats,
People wearing scarves,
People wearing winter coats.

Sarah Rossiter (10)
Donwell Primary School

FAMILIES AND FRIENDS

Meet the new boy I know,
Auntie Mary says go,
Mammy says come here noo,
Mandy knows he loves Winnie The Pooh
Andy is his friend,
Laura kindly lends
Sara loves him very much,
So does Uncle Butch.

Kimberley Ampleford (11)
Donwell Primary School

SORE BELLY

There was a girl called Kelly,
Who had a very sore belly.
She went to the shop,
And bought some pop,
And then she ate some jelly.

Her mother said
'Get back into bed'
You're very sick my dear
She cried one lonely tear
The next day she lay dead.

Kelly Ball (11)
Donwell Primary School

SKIPPY DIPPY

Skippy is a dippy newt,
Who, to others is a whiz,
To girls, he is cute,
To us he is a newt,
Who enjoys surfing the fizz.

He is a cool guy who surfs every hour,
Who can rip up waves with amazing power,
He always gets first prize,
In every surfing competition,
And catches everyone's eyes.

Luke Torr (9)
Donwell Primary School

ALPHABET

A is for Aunty author Ann
B is for brother builder Ben
C is for cousin calculator Carl
D is for daughter digger Danielle
E is for empty Elena egg
F is for fatty Fireman Fred
G is for gambler Greg greengrocer
H is for hungry halfmoon Harry
I is for idiot ill Ian
J is for jumpy Jack
K is for Kim kickboxer
L is for Liam lamb licker
M is for Melinie mental mad woman
N is for naughty nightwalker Ned
O is for Owen ocean opener
P is for Peter pockey pick-pocket
Q is for Queeny quidsnacker
R is for hot rod Rocky
S is for sneaky stalker Smith
T is for Tena tiny toe
U is for Umpfrey unhelpful
V is for Valery very small
W is for Wayhn waddling, wallaby
X is for Xena Xylophone
Y is for Yena yeti
Z is for Zac zebra.

Danielle Nelson (10)
Donwell Primary School

ABC . . .

A is for Annie who bites her nails,
B is for Bobery who pulls dogs tails,
C is for Cara who eats boiled cats,
D is for Dora who executes rats,
E is for Edwina who swallows mud,
F is for Fredrick who smells of rose buds,
G is for Gregory who has chubby cheeks,
H is for Harriet who absolutely reeks!
I is for Isabel who hates having baths,
J is for Johnny who strangely loves maths!
K is for Kerry who has a runny nose,
L is for Luke who has no toes,
M is for Miranda who loves netball,
N is for Nathan who is very tall,
O is for Otto who has ear wax,
P is for Penny who whacks with an axe,
Q is for Quentin who never washes his hair,
R is for Randy who stamps on a chair,
S is for Samuel who always gets a clout,
T is for Timothy who is very stout,
U is for Umphrey who hates staying put,
V is for Valerie who has a crazy haircut,
W is for Willamina who sniffs tomato tins
X is for Xippy who plays in the bins,
Y is for Yolanda who always cries,
Z is for Zacious who waves goodbye.

Miranda Sheehy (9)
Donwell Primary School

THE T-REX

One huge step
One mighty roar
One swoop of the tail
One swipe of the claw.

Two fierce eyes
Two expert ears
Two strong legs
Two clever ideas.

Three things on his mind
Three goals for his day
Three delicious meals
Three seconds to run away.
    Ahhhhhh!

Lucy Gibson (9)
Donwell Primary School

NAUGHTY WAYNE

There was once a boy called Wayne,
He was getting to be a pain,
He jumped around like a lunatic,
He killed his poor Uncle Mick,
His teacher flies an aeroplane.

He hates everyone who hangs around,
He tries to get them with his greyhound,
His uncle is a maniac,
Another maniac is Jack,
He hates to hear a noisy sound.

Wayne Heathwaite (11)
Donwell Primary School

MY LIFE

M any years I've been living
Y ear after year I've been naughty.

L ie after lie I've been wrong
I is for idiot for doing bad things
F is for football which is my favourite hobby
E is for the nice estate I live in!

Thomas Clements (10)
Donwell Primary School

DIFFERENT COLOURS

Red is like our red handle that ticks,
Red is like blood when you pick.
Orange is like the waddling feet of a duck.
Orange is like my face when I get stuck in the muck.
Purple is like my mum's coat.
Purple is like that boat in the sea.

Katie Stokoe (8)
Donwell Primary School

SATAN

Between the fire is the most powerful power,
The powers so strong it makes people cower.
The power comes from only one man,
The power hits with a deafening bang.

It's bright red and under the ground,
He screeches in a high pitched sound,
The sound is one you've never heard,
It sounds a bit like an injured bird.

Paul Gallagher (10)
Donwell Primary School

THE MOON

Moon shines brightly,
Moon is cheese,
Moon is freezing,
Moon is a face.

Moon is bright white,
Moon is in the air,
Moon is a football,
Moon shines upon us.

Moon floats nicely,
Moon is a circle,
Moon is quiet,
Man in the moon.

Nadine Barrett (9)
Donwell Primary School

WHY?

Why do I have to go to school?
Why can't I go to the swimming pool?
And why not go to George's house
To watch him swallow Mike the mouse?

Why can't you be nice to me?
And fix me up a cup of tea?
And why can't I wear a tie, just like a guy?
Can I ask you a question?

Why?

Sean Watson (11)
Donwell Primary School

A FROSTY WINTER

As I cross the road for school
I see people all ready for winter.

I see people building snowmen
Having a really good time.

I see people with funny hats
With bobbly bits on top.

I see people laughing and throwing
big round snowballs.

I see people with mums,
dads and family.

Kelsey Abbas (10)
Donwell Primary School

SWEETS

S weets, sweets, yum, yum, yum,
W ish I had some for my tum,
E ating them all day long,
E xcellently chosen by me
T ooth rotting is not to be,
S weets, sweets, yum, yum, yum.

Laura Greener (10)
Donwell Primary School

FOOTBALL MANIAC!

F   is for feet
O   is for opportunity
O   is for own goal
T   is for talent
B   is for ball
A   is for amazing
L   is for linesmen
L   is for lightning.

Michael Campbell (10)
Donwell Primary School

STORM

As the lightning strikes down
It makes a crashing noise.
Its flash is like
A torch from the clouds,
And the rain is like
Tears from someone who has been crying.
The lightning is as blue as the sea.

Jake Sherring (10)
Donwell Primary School

A STORM ON THE SEA

The storm has come,
And stretched his mighty fingers.
The waves are crashing,
The lightning flashing,
And the moon has gone to bed.
Another day is yet to come.

Louise Devlin (10)
Donwell Primary School

MY CAT!

As she whisks her silky tail,
She gives a cry, a waily wail,
Eyes like beads that watch the clock,
She dances to the beat, tick-tock.

The clock meets the hour, she prepares to leap,
But the hidden bird has time to keep,
With claws outstretched, she jumps in the air,
But once again, her prey just isn't there!

Jenna Gray (10)
Donwell Primary School

LIMERICK

There was a young boy called Shaun,
Who loved to eat prawns,
He goes on holiday to Spain,
And his parents think he is a pain.
He always likes to beep his horn.

Shaun Lowden (11)
Donwell Primary School

PAUL

There was a young boy called Paul,
Which had to jump over a wall,
In less than a call,
Paul was very tall,
So he was too big to fit through the door, the next day.

Nathan Duffy (10)
Donwell Primary School

THE MOON

Look in the sky,
There's a big, orange pie.

Look, you can see,
But that cannot be.

It's a ball,
But it's bigger than the mall.

It's too round to be a lace,
But it's just right for a face.

If that's true,
Would it say *boo!*

Jordan Pollington (9)
Donwell Primary School

AUTUMN MONSTER

Lock your windows
Shut your doors,
Switch your lights on,
Before the autumn monster gets you.
He's got leaves all over him,
Strong as well,
Legs as strong as steel,
So lock your doors.

Peter McGrath (10)
Donwell Primary School

BUILDING SITE

Heave and ho
To and fro
Crashing into buildings,
Chimneys toppling over,
Squashing people all day.

Heave and ho
To and fro,
Pumping, pumping,
Pumping, pumping,
People up
All day,
To and fro.

Luke Corkin (9)
Donwell Primary School

I WISH!

I wish I was a singer,
A pop star for the world to see
I wish I was a health back bringer,
Like a nurse to cure someone's knee!

I wish I could just stay myself,
And if I could you'd see,
All day I would enjoy myself,
Just all my friends and me!

Lisa Collins (10)
Donwell Primary School

SEASONS

Spring
As spring starts, bulbs begin to rise
Baby birds start to fly in the skies.

Summer
We look forward to summer sun,
Ice cream, holidays and having fun.
We like being off school
To play in the pool.

Autumn
The green leaves turn to red and brown
As autumn approaches I have a frown.
Early dark nights and windy days
The wind howls and blows things different ways.

Winter
The weather gets cold to let us know
We might be in for some winter snow
At least we know that Christmas is not long to go.

Katie Robinson (7)
Donwell Primary School

THE SUN

I come from the light
I am way up in the sky
I can see everything
I dry up everything in my sight
I go down at night.

Christopher Richardson (10)
Donwell Primary School

CATS

Hello I am a cat
My name is Scat.
Cats are cool
Cats rule, dogs drool
Cats lie on mats
Cats chase bats
Cats like to be upstairs
And go to sleep on chairs.
They like to be on the bed
They love to be fed.

Lucinda Gray (8)
Donwell Primary School

A WINTER'S NIGHT

On a cold winter's night,
You can see the moonlight,
Next to the sparkling stars.

As the moon goes to sleep,
And the hills go steep,
The birds sing to the sheep.

Now up comes the sun
Down goes the moon,
It's time for fun.

Fahd Al-Hooti (10)
Donwell Primary School

CHRISTMASTIME

Running, playing, sledging, fun,
Cocoa, hot fire, building fun,
Snowballs, Christmas, Santa, fun,
Snowblankets, snowmen, presents, fun.

Snowflakes fall past my window,
The winds whispering to get in,
I wake up in the morning,
Oh look Santa's been.

Running, playing, sledging, fun,
Cocoa, hot fire, building, fun,
Snowmen, snow blankets, presents, fun
Snowballs, Christmas, Santa,
    Fun!

Stephanie Hall (9)
Donwell Primary School

THE WIND

The wind swirls round in circles,
As his hands pick packets up
And waves them around in the air.

He blows people's hats off
And he loves to dance round people.
So he can blow them away.

Gemma Horn (10)
Donwell Primary School

THE LUNCHTIME

It's twelve o'clock, line up at the door
Run downstairs to the hall floor.
I hope it's curry
So let's hurry
I go outside to have some fun
Running around *eating* a bun.
Fell in the mud
That felt good
It's one o'clock, go to get my books
Giving dirty looks.

Claire Smiles (9)
Donwell Primary School

THE WINDY NIGHT

The wind whooshes
at my window
every night when
I go to bed.

The wind swoops
and goes round in swirls.

The wind is so cold,
it's coming around
the corner
right about now!

David King (10)
Donwell Primary School

MY BIRTHDAY

My birthday is very great
I like to play with my mate.
I like my red jelly
And when you get a fat belly.
We play lots of games
And the clowns call us silly names.
At my birthday I got something to make
And my mam bought me a cake.
My friends had a good cry
When I went to say goodbye.

Lucy Marshall (7)
Donwell Primary School

WILDFIRE

Wildfire is as hot as the sun
And it spreads like butter across the forest.
As it crackles around the forest,
It destroys everything it wants to.
One minute you see a beautiful green forest
Next you see a pile of burning smoky ashes.

Max Brown (10)
Donwell Primary School

THE WINTER

Snowflakes sprinkle a frosty scent,
Icicles hang on your nose,
As you walk upon the grass,
It begins to snow.

Samantha Spencer (9)
Donwell Primary School

A HOT DESERT IN EGYPT

The sun is sizzling
Over the land,
Everything is hot
Isn't a plant in sight.

Tall pyramids,
Bright blue sky,
Sand as soft as silk,
Egypt has a sunset.

Laura Winder (9)
Donwell Primary School

ANIMALS AND JELLY

I have a dog
It smells like a hog.
I have a lazy cat
Because it sleeps on the mat.
When I eat jelly
I get a fat belly.

Luke Garbutt (7)
Donwell Primary School

COLOUR POEM

Blue is like the brightest sky
Blue is like the wings of a fly
Blue is like the deep deep sea
Crashing and waving on my friends and me.

Craig Johnson (8)
Donwell Primary School

MY BIRTHDAY

My birthday is great
I see all my mates.
We all eat jelly
We get a big belly.
We play lots of games
Then we call out the names.
My mum always bakes
I have a giant cake.
We all cry
When we have to say bye.
I'll see you next time
Don't do any crimes!

Mark Clapp (8)
Donwell Primary School

SPRINGTIME

Flowers lie like blankets on the ground,
Petals, open one by one,
Blossom hangs like popcorn on trees,
Time to pick daffodils!

Chicks hatch from their eggs
Lambs bounce like trampolinists,
It's time to open our eggs
    Springtime!

Zoë Bulch (10)
Donwell Primary School

MY BIRTHDAY

My birthday is great,
I see all my mates.
I love all the jelly,
I love it to my belly.
I love my new things,
I feel great when they sing.
We play lots of games,
I have a friend called James.
My mum bakes,
All my fairy cakes.

Jessica Tonge (7)
Donwell Primary School

POSTERS

Posters are *big* and *bold*
They *warn* people about lots of things
They *warn* people about things like:
Danger
Electricity
Deep water
Hot things
Water
Roads
So always read posters
And keep yourself safe.

Joe Albert (7)
Donwell Primary School

What Is Yellow?

Yellow is the aroma of the sun
sizzling and frying people in a heatwave.

Yellow is the beauty of winning a million pounds
on Who Wants To Be A Millionaire?

Yellow is the bouquet of bananas hanging on a
tropical island in the sunshine.

Yellow is the sight of the rippling sea
on a hot breezy day.

Steven Hodgson (9)
Glebe Village Primary School

Witch's Spell

Human lung and heart of dog,
Piglet's liver and slime of frog,
Eye of cod and whisker of cat
Oyster's pearl and stomach of rat,
Tooth of tiger, giant wasp's sting,
Spine of badger and eagle's wing.

Chorus
Bubble, bubble, rock and stubble,
Cauldron burn and hell broth bubble,
Fire, fire, grow and grow,
The drinker of this both will be no more!

David Wilson
Glebe Village Primary School

WHAT IS ORANGE?

Orange is the flavour of mangoes
squeezed hard and tight.

Orange is the perfume of daffodils
as they sway gentle, summer breeze.

Orange is the taste of sizzling,
hot cinder toffee spitting out of a
volcano when it erupts.

Orange is the aroma of buttercups
tossing their heads in the breeze.

Orange is the taste of juicy tangerines
eaten on a balmy, summer's evening.

Orange is the fragrance of fresh fruit on
a beautiful summer's evening.

Orange is the sight of women wearing dresses
on a warm evening.

Orange is the aroma of peaches
ripening on trees in the orchards of Spain.

Julie Bell (10)
Glebe Village Primary School

STARS

All through the night stars gaze down upon us,
As we sleep the stars whisper to each other.
The stars dance in the night sky and sparkle like
                                    little diamonds,
All night the stars look like little sequins on a
                                    black quilt.

Kirsty English (10)
Glebe Village Primary School

WITCH'S SPELL

A rabbit's ear, a rat's tail,
A raven's feather, a bat on a rail,
Slow snail's slime, a tasty slug,
A spider's leg, a juicy bug,
A beak from a duck, a dog's coat,
A scale from a dragon the size of a boat.

Chorus
Round and round the potion goes,
All he needs is one small dose,
bubble and rise, bubble and rise,
Thou who makes Macbeth suffer dies.

Amy Hoogewerf (11)
Glebe Village Primary School

SPACE

Space, space! we forgot our suitcase
How many times has the moon had a face
The dog called Tiati is in a race
He is in space
He could be dead
And needs to be fed
He broke the table
We should have kept him in a stable
He might get a fright
He might fly round a satellite.

Andrew Green (9)
Glebe Village Primary School

MOON

We went to the moon
on a dark dark night.
An asteroid tried to kill us.
He did not need to kill me.
I nearly died when he shot his space gun.
Out he came from beneath the ground
looking scary all around
scaring the life out of me.

Sam Witherspoon (8)
Glebe Village Primary School

FIRE

Fire is an orangey purple light bulb.
He jumps and leaps, leaving a trail of blazing flames
                            wherever it travels.
He reaches around to find something new to ignite.
He licks anything it can find, fiercely and furiously.
He is a burning devil!

Jamie McIntyre
Glebe Village Primary School

POETRY

Shooting stars fly through the night
The moon is glittering silver,
And shines through midnight.

The Earth is green and blue,
Green means plants and blue means seas.
And this is the poem you will not forget?

Christopher McGrath (9)
Glebe Village Primary School

THE SUN

He is a huge shining orb
which strolls across the enormous sky.
He is a giant yellow beach ball that
floats in the creamy-blue summer sky.
He is a huge light bulb which sends his rays
to the green sphere shaped Earth.
He spreads his beams across the Earth
to give it warmth and light,
He nurtures the Earth.

Carl Lockey (11)
Glebe Village Primary School

THE VILLAGE WITH NO NAME

Dreadful trolls charging slowly
Sickening vampires biting horribly
Dirty aliens sucking disgustingly
in the village with no name.

Scary monsters eating dangerously
Ugly goblins grabbing sluggishly
Tiny oompa lumpas shopping hurriedly
in the village with no name.

Pale giants stomping noisily
Chubby crocodiles snapping quickly
Dead zombies sleepwalking steadily
in the village with no name.

Spotty witches casting madly
Hairy people dancing beastly
Giant worms digging viciously
in the village with no name.

Courtney Wright (9)
Grange Park Primary School

THE VILLAGE WITH NO NAME

Enormous dragons fighting frightfully,
Vicious trolls attacking deadly
Hideous aliens attacking fearsomely.
In the village with no name.

Ugly zombies sucking fearfully
Spotty mummies catching quickly
Gruesome rats nibbling horribly
In the village with no name.

Oozy goblins biting dreadfully
Repulsive vampires sucking disgustingly
Vicious spiders, spinning gangly
In the village with no name.

Milky white ghosts flying secretly
Toffee teddy bears sticking slowly
Warty witches flying quickly
In the village with no name.

Rebecca Barnes (8)
Grange Park Primary School

THE VILLAGE WITH NO NAME

Bloodsucking vampires biting viciously
Frightening dragons blowing fire quickly
Gory raptors eating swiftly
In the village with no name.

Slimy snakes sliding scarily
Huge goblins creeping quietly
Oozy aliens shooting quickly
In the village with no name.

Ugly witches casting spells quickly
Spooky ghosts flying high
Scary mummies running quickly
In the village with no name.

Ugly trolls jogging slowly
Titchy bats flying swiftly
Smelly dogs fighting viciously
In the village with no name.

Graeme Loughlin (8)
Grange Park Primary School

THE VILLAGE WITH NO NAME

Hairy primates howling loudly
Creepy mummies rolling quickly
Plump ox plus horse eater running firmly
In the village with no name.

Parky dragons digging furiously
Sucking trolls eating wickedly
Bloodthirsty tarantulas crawling wildly
In the village with no name.

Unfair zombies coming slobbily
Sick goblins crawling slowly
Noisy skeletons storming powerfully
In the village with no name.

Poorly witches spelling crazily
Disgusting ghosts swinging quickly
Quiet worms chewing slowly
In the village with no name.

Marc Jenkinson (8)
Grange Park Primary School

THE VILLAGE WITH NO NAME

Oozy aliens roasting viciously
Ugly trolls running slowly
Bloodsucking vampires biting quickly
In the village with no name.

Man-eating flies eating viciously
Dirty gremlins leaping quietly,
Tall bears charging quickly
In the village with no name.

Slimy bugs sucking horribly
Long crocodiles biting noisily
Gooey nits biting noisily
In the village with no name.

Groovy worms dancing viciously
Nasty wizards zapping dangerously
Dotty witches eating slowly
In the village with no name.

Adam Hepple (9)
Grange Park Primary School

THE VILLAGE WITH NO NAME

Spooky ghosts flying secretly
Ugly trolls walking creepily
Warty witches flying creepily
In the village with no name.

Gruesome vampires biting scarily
Angry zombies crawling crappily
Gory mummies eating viciously
In the village with no name.

Giant dragons breathing quickly
Tiny aliens biting deadly
Enormous bats flying gracefully
In the village with no name.

Ugly gremlins casting wickedly
Hairy spiders crawling easily
Dead people hunting hardly
In the village with no name.

Taylor Davies (9)
Grange Park Primary School

THE VILLAGE WITH NO NAME

Enormous slug attacking disgustingly
Disgusting trolls squashing viciously
Vikings fighting viciously
In the village with no name.

Huge bats frightening secretly
Slimy snakes crawling gushingly
Titchy rats nibbling viciously
In the village with no name.

Enormous spiders crawling disgustingly
Great dragons flying high
Little goblins running quickly
In the village with no name.

Ugly witches casting spells secretly
Enormous spiders crawling slowly
Bulky giants running quickly
In the village with no name.

Ashleigh Burlinson (8)
Grange Park Primary School

THE VILLAGE WITH NO NAME

Stupid trolls running slowly
Enormous bone crunchers crumbling viciously
Oozy aliens sucking preciously
In the village with no name.

Vicious vampires munching horribly
Eerie zombies scattering quickly
Fast werewolves jumping weirdly
In the village with no name.

Giant snot monsters munching disgustingly
Considerable demons sleepwalking stupidly
Squalid mummies walking weirdly
In the village with no name.

Angry bats beating slowly
Spooky rats running quietly
Stupid goblins turning slimely
In the village with no name.

Jonathan Peverley (8)
Grange Park Primary School

THE VILLAGE WITH NO NAME

Colossal trolls burping violently
Stupid aliens flying weirdly
Enormous cyclops crushing viciously
In the village with no name.

Hairy werewolves howling loudly
Dead zombies eating disgustingly
Bony skeletons sleepwalking sleepily
In the village with no name.

Giant teddies sleeping deeply
Scary witches flying eerily,
Dumb vampires biting rapidly
In the village with no name.

Slimy serpents swimming stealthily
Green dragons flaming quickly
Enormous griffins clawing wildly
In the village with no name.

Bobby Ewart (8)
Grange Park Primary School

THE VILLAGE WITH NO NAME

Oozy aliens shooting dangerously,
Unattractive trolls digging quickly,
Man-eating rats biting viciously
In the village with no name.

Microscopic vampires sucking badly,
Giant worms digging deeply
Dotty witches eating slowly
In the village with no name.

Nasty wizards zapping nastily
Gooey toffee monsters munching quickly
Hairy giants sleeping loudly
In the village with no name.

Slimy bugs sucking horribly
Long crocodiles biting nastily
Dirty frogs leaping quickly
In the village with no name.

Nathan Conlin (9)
Grange Park Primary School

THE VILLAGE WITH NO NAME

Enormous rats attacking deadly
Trifling trolls fighting viciously
Oozy man-eating birds snapping sharply
In the village with no name.

Hideous aliens biting disgustingly
Spotty mummies scaring frighteningly
Sucking dragons breathing fire horribly
In the village with no name.

Sick vampires eating quickly
Green umperlumpers kicking hardly
Dead people lying flatly
In the village with no name.

Gloomy skeletons walking slowly
Toffee monsters slaying disgustingly
Jelly bears swallowing badly
In the village with no name.

Jessica Richardson (8)
Grange Park Primary School

THE VILLAGE WITH NO NAME

Large mummies stomping loudly
Minute goblins biting viciously
Colossal ghosts flying spookily
In the village with no name.

Massive zombies killing slowly
Slimy aliens shooting dangerously
Gooey man-eating rats scuttling quickly
In the village with no name.

Fat giants walking noisily
Scary gremlins screeching quickly
Spooky witches cackling wildly
In the village with no name.

Bulky dragons breathing fiercely
Freaky wizards spelling weirdly
Bony skeletons walking quietly
In the village with no name.

Nicolle Braddick (8)
Grange Park Primary School

THEE VILLAGE WITH NO NAME

Ginormous vampires sucking noisily
Man-eating fish eating messily
Oozy UFO's whizzing crazily
In the village with no name.

Huge dragons flying gently
Massive zombies chasing quickly
Giant mummies chasing quietly
In the village with no name.

Man-eating birds eating wildly
Man-eating parrots eating sloppily
Large wizards spelling scarily
In the village with no name.

Huge goblins eating messily
Large skeletons clicking noisily
Huge witches spelling quickly
In the village with no name.

James Cowie (8)
Grange Park Primary School

THE VILLAGE WITH NO NAME

Gory mummies attacking fearfully
Enormous bats sucking loudly
Gruesome zombies killing quickly
In the village with no name.

Tiny aliens fighting viciously
Ugly rats biting deadly
Oozy vampires killing fearfully
In the village with no name.

Strong bone crunchers crunching loudly
Giant dragons breathing quickly
Noisy gremlins screaming noisily
In the village with no name.

Warty witches hunting secretly
Massive ghosts flying quickly
Spooky spiders crawling slowly
In the village with no name.

Liam Anderson (8)
Grange Park Primary School

THE VILLAGE WITH NO NAME

Deadly people killing nastily
Wizardy wizards spell nastily
Horny cyclops ripping deadly
In the village with no name.

Ugly aliens zapping quickly
Scary dragons killing slowly
Hissing snakes slithering slowly
In the village with no name.

Dead mummies dancing slowly
Swooping eagles flying quickly
Warty witches laughing horribly
In the village with no name.

Alive cars walking slowly
Deadly dinosaur biting slowly
Scary ghosts scaring horribly
In the village with no name.

Aidan Potts (8)
Grange Park Primary School

THE VILLAGE WITH NO NAME

Slimy aliens eating viciously
Creepy vampires bleeding uncaringly
Bony skeletons clicking madly
In the village with no name.

Dirty witches flying wickedly
Roaring dragons swooping faintly
Sleepy zombies dreaming excitedly
In the village with no name.

Hairy spiders spinning dizzily
Hissing snakes slithering slowly
Tired umpa-lumpahs dozing sleepily
In the village with no name.

Vicious bulldogs snapping bravely
Stupid wizards relaxing lazily
Amazing goblins stomping nervously
In the village with no name.

Kassie Rennoldson (7)
Grange Park Primary School

THE VILLAGE WITH NO NAME

Enormous monsters destroying angrily
Stray dogs barking viciously
Ragged goblins screaming loudly
In the village with no name.

Squelchy rats talking quietly
Oozy umperlumpers dancing funnily
Smelly jumper beans hopping quickly
In the village with no name.

Babbling babies talking snappily
Smelling ghosts floating sneakily
Snapping croakers snapping crunchingly
In the village with no name.

Poisonous snakes hissing terribly
Slimy mummies dancing dreadfully
Clever vampires shooting wildly
In the village with no name.

Kirsty Heffernan (9)
Grange Park Primary School

THE VILLAGE WITH NO NAME

Scary mummies walking horribly
Monstrous monsters attacking viciously
Slimy aliens playing happily
In the village with no name.

Evil witches laughing horribly
Hulking trolls growling ghastly
Stupid wizards experimenting slowly
In the village with no name.

Oozy vampires kicking darkly
Horrible zombies running madly
Weary skeletons sleepwalking sleepily
In the village with no name.

Painful rats lying tiredly
Sneaky bats flying highly
Oozy bone crunchers crunching happily
In the village with no name.

Lucy Tarn (7)
Grange Park Primary School

THE VILLAGE WITH NO NAME

Hairy trolls battling viciously
Wrapped up mummies attack powerfully
White ghosts play happily
In the village with no name.

Black witches cast spells skilfully
Oozy cyclops speak unhappily
Red devils poke sneakily
In the village with no name.

Ravenous snakes slither quickly
Skilled wizards curse properly
Black cats scratch painfully
In the village with no name.

Tiny bats flutter highly
Enormous dragons fly easily
Hot tassilisks turn people to stone smoothly
In the village with no name.

Nicole Eden (8)
Grange Park Primary School

TEN THINGS FOUND IN AN ASTRONAUT'S POCKET

1 Jupiter's black hole
2 A forbidden galaxy
3 Flames from the sun
4 Half of an 'In Space Map'
5 A dozen filters of oxygen
6 Starship Troopers computer game
7 A silver wrapper from a Kit Kat
8 The North Star
9 A pair of extra powerful space booster boots
10 A giant letter from Neil Armstrong.

Scott Renney (10)
Harraton Primary School

TEN THINGS IN A BUSY MUM'S POCKET

1   Red square cloth
2   A large bottle of washing up liquid
3   A voomy long hoover
4   A large bottle of polish
5   An unusually long tin of air freshener
6   A terribly smelly bottle of bleach
7   A tiny tin of window cleaner
8   A blue square wet cloth
9   A compact mobile phone
10 A sizeable pen wrapped with blue square cloth.

Curtis Connor (10)
Harraton Primary School

THE HURRICANE

It whisks along the ground,
And scoops everything away
With its enormous hands.
It leaves nothing unturned,
Kicks down trees,
As it scoops up the ruins.
Then as it moves away,
It leaves the broken down earth
                to rebuild.

Sarah Crossling (10)
Harraton Primary School

TEN THINGS LOST IN A RUNAWAY CHILD'S POCKET

A lovely glossy picture of the place that they are going to
A couple of hundred pounds for food
A very old teddy to hug and to love
A car to drive to my dreams.
A pair of knickers and socks
A two day old sandwich
A quite recent photo of Mam and Dad
Half a pint of milk
A mouldy chocolate bar
A snotty handkerchief.

Hannah Greenhow (11)
Harraton Primary School

NIGHT

Owls hooting in the darkness of night
Rats scurrying about near the dustbins
Trees casting gloomy shadows over houses
The dark sky, dark as the darkest castle.
Bats gliding through the blackness
Haunted house with spooky ghosts swinging around
                                    the towers.
Zombies trailing along the ground
Clouds full of thunder and lightning
In the darkness of the night.

Touran Parsee (10)
Mill Hill School

LOOKING OUT OF MY WINDOW

I stand at my window
All I see is the moon glistening
It looks as if it's coming closer.

The stars are twinkling
Like big bright jewels.

The air smells fresh and clean,
The streets are all free of rubbish
As if a fairy had just been.

The white fluffy clouds
Running into each other
Forming pictures in the sky.

I close the curtains
And snuggle up in my nice warm bed
Dreaming of what tomorrow night will bring.

Natalie Moore (10)
Mill Hill School

HAPPINESS

Happiness is yellow and gold
Happiness tastes like fresh orange juice
Happiness smells like a red rose
Happiness looks like a hot summer's day with
children playing in a yard.
Happiness sounds like a calm ocean
Happiness feels like a peaceful day.

Stephanie Small (10)
Mill Hill School

MIDNIGHT ANIMALS

I jumped out of bed
tiptoeing
to my open window.

I see black cats
staring
with tiny yellow eyes.

Bats gliding over trees
swaying
in the bitter cold night.

Dogs behind thorn bushes
whimpering
with pain and fear.

Owls hovering over the grass
hunting
eyes looking for their supper.

Rats scuttering around
chasing
tiny fat insects.

Standing at my open window
watching
I silently tiptoed back to bed.

Vanessa Wilkinson (9)
Mill Hill School

Out In The Darkness

As I stood outside on my doorstep
The night was
As black as a tree in the darkness.
It was as cold as ice.

The owl perched on top of a bare tree
It cried out for some food.

I saw a shadow of
a sly old fox shivering
as he slinked home with his prey.

The mice were cold and frightened
They huddled together
In the darkness of their small home.

The badgers creep back home
To keep out of the bitter cold.

I slowly disappeared back into my house
And crept upstairs to my warm, cosy bed.

Victoria Prentice (10)
Mill Hill School

Yuk!

Wake up, moan,
Open my eyes, groan,
Monday morning,
Yuk!

Into the bathroom,
Splish, splash, splosh,
Monday morning,
Yuk!

Drag myself downstairs,
Cereal crunch, toast munch,
Monday morning,
Yuk!

Clothes on, shoes on,
Out the door *Bang!*
Monday morning,
Yuk!
Yuk!
Yuk!

Melissa Gunn (10)
Mill Hill School

THERE'S SOMEONE IN MY BEDROOM

Lying in my bed,
Not daring to move
It feels like someone's watching me,
Watching every move my eyeballs make.

I can't figure out who it is,
Or what it is!
Is it an alien from outer space?
Or is it a monster from inside the cupboard?
I dare to move!
I move my legs,
Then my arms,
Then make for the door,
I'm about to scream -

I feel a tap on my shoulder,
I turn around,
It's only my big brother!

Rachel Charlton (10)
Mill Hill School

AS SCARY AS NIGHT

I was lying in my bed
at dead of night.
Suddenly!
I heard a really spooky noise.
My body tensed
I lay as still as . . .
I didn't dare move.
Suddenly!
Footsteps creaked slowly upstairs.
I tried to scream
but nothing came out.
Suddenly!
The light came on
as bright . . .
Who had come in my room?
Only my dad to say, 'Goodnight.'

Kirstie Robertson (10)
Mill Hill School

WHAT'S IN THE BLACKNESS OF NIGHT

I look into the blackness of night but . . .
What do I see?
I see nothing.

What do I hear?
I hear the cats as they prowl around
The dogs as they howl at the moon
Which shines from gold to silver as it creeps
By the misty night sky.

I hear the sound of people talking.
I hear field mice scampering around,
I hear cars quickly going by.

Why don't I see anything when I look out into
The blackness of the night sky?

Chloe McCabe (9)
Mill Hill School

NIGHT STRIKES TWELVE

I was in bed, in the countryside when
Bang!
It was the clock striking twelve.
Then shadows, appearing from nowhere, could be seen
I was scared stiff.

I dare not move in case a ghost grabbed me.
Creek . . . creek . . .
The door handle moves.
Try not to be scared.
I'm a boy aged ten!
I'm not scared of the dark!

The curtains blow.
My heart beats
Dum . . . Dum . . . Dum!

I feel my toe getting played with.
I shout, 'Mam, Dad, I'm scared stiff.'
'Go to sleep' they say.

So I get my torch
And fall asleep, finally.

Adam Williamson (9)
Mill Hill School

I WAKE UP!

I wake up
Aaarrreee!
I get out of bed
Bang!
I go to the toilet
cchhhh!
I get a shower
Shhhh!
I go downstairs
Stammmpp!

The toaster goes
Pooooof!
My dad goes to work
Brum! Brum!
I eat my breakfast
Snap! Crackle! Pop!
And me.
Me I have to go to school
Aarreee! M   annn!

Keith Watson (10)
Mill Hill School

MIDNIGHT

The clock strikes midnight
Shadows appear everywhere.
Trees swaying in the wind
Rain pattering on the windowpane
Owls flying in the night sky.

The moon glistening on the houses
Gates creaking
Rats squeaking
In the middle of the night.

Darker than shadows
Darker than trees
As black as a bat
As black as a cat
In the middle of the night.

Philippa Liddle (10)
Mill Hill School

OFF WE GO TO SCHOOL AGAIN

Off we go to school.
Rrrrorrorr
Alarm clock goes off
Ring, ring, ring.
Having a horrible wash
Rubbing and scrubbing
Splishing and splashing.
Off goes the kettle
Eeeekkkk.
The butter dribbles down my chin
Whiddley diddley.
Ghosts howling in the wind
Whoooooo
Mum making breakfast
Rruummbblee.
I eat my lunch,
Munch, crunch.
I go to the toilet
Shhhhhh
And off we go to school.
Oh man!

Kieran Lowe (10)
Mill Hill School

IMAGES OF MY WORLD

Night is a sleeping sky
With twinkling, glistening stars.
Everything is as still as a sleeping bat
It is as quiet as an empty room.

The grass is a green carpet
Blowing softly in the breeze,
Making a calm soft noise of air.

The sea is a mat of cold,
It is never-ending and it is
a deep blue water pump.

David Armstrong (9)
Mill Hill School

FRIENDSHIP

Friendship makes me feel warm
Like the golden rays of the sun,
playing gently on my face.

Friendship reminds me of everything good
Like delicious strawberry ice cream
on a hot summer's afternoon.

Friendship to me is a diamond ring
To be prized and treasured
for its strength and value.

Hayley Porter (9)
Mill Hill School

THE JUNGLE'S BLACKNESS IN THE DARK, DARK CITY

Rain lashes against the pavement.

Cars look like lizards
The headlights of cars are as bright
as a full moon and shine in the darkness.

Everything is as black as space.

Houses look like giant monsters.

Motorbikes grin as their noise attacks
                        everything in sight.

The dead of night
scares everyone away.

Everything looks the same.

Everything melts away when the sun
                        comes up again.

Adam Clark (9)
Mill Hill School

FRIENDSHIP

Friendship is orange
Friendship tastes like a juicy sweet pear.
Friendship smells like fresh flowers growing
                        in the fields.
Friendship looks like a big bird with glittering wings.
Friendship soulds like the wind blowing through the trees.
Friendship feels like laying on a hot sunny beach.

Sophie Teer (10)
Mill Hill School

MONDAY MORNING

Dawn struck
I get out of bed yawning
And I mumbled Yuk!
It's school!
I stomped downstairs
Dragging my feet along
I sank into one of the chairs
Gulping my breakfast down.
When I finished my breakfast
I ran into the lounge.
Then suddenly I started to cough!
When I had stopped coughing
I was going upstairs to brush my teeth.
I wasn't looking where I was going
Then I accidentally bumped into my brother Keith.
Putting my toothbrush back
With a rub-a-dub-dub I started to wash my face.
Combing my hair down, shur, shur.
Looking into my bookcase,
To find my reading book.
Found it!
Quickly run downstairs
And off
    I run
        to
           school.

Rebecca Swales (9)
Mill Hill School

TRICKS OF THE NIGHT

As the cat sits on the gloomy fence,
And me in my bed my body all tense.
I fear that I'm not alone,
Just then I hear a grunt and groan.
A monster!
A bear!
Or even a dragon!
Suddenly I hear the wheels of a wagon
But then, it goes quiet, in my big, dark house.
I can't even hear the squeaking of a mouse
Finally I shut my eyes tight.
It was only the tricks of the dark, silent night
Or was it?

Melanie Blakemore (10)
Mill Hill School

NIGHT

Night is like . . .
A bee
Hiding from the world.

Night is like . . .
A lonely fox
Strolling on its own.

Night is like . . .
A dark gloomy attic
With no windows.

Amy Brown (9)
Mill Hill School

MUSIC

Music is yours
Music is mine
Music is for everyone
All of the time.

Music is happy
Music is sad
Music can sometimes
Make you feel mad.

Music is cool!
Music is fun!
Music is good
When you're out in the sun.

Music comes
Music goes
But where to?
Nobody knows.

Rachael Briton (9)
Mill Hill School

LONELINESS IS . . .

Loneliness is black.
Loneliness tastes like a soggy apricot.
Loneliness smells like a weed.
Loneliness looks like a new child looking for
                            someone to play with.
Loneliness sounds like a dark, silent night.
Loneliness feels like you're the only one in the world.

Megan Tedder (9)
Mill Hill School

A School Morning

Out of bed
I bashed my head *oouucchhh!*
On the bedside table *Bang!*
My dog Mable
Ate my bagel *oonooo!*
And hid under the kitchen table.
I hate to say this but I can't wait to get
to school.
Even though I hate Mr Pool!

Meggan Tansey (9)
Mill Hill School

Funny

Funny is sky blue, pink with yellow dots.
Funny tastes like sherbet fizzing on your tongue.
Funny smells like strawberry flavoured sprouts.
Funny looks like a clown juggling three cats and two dogs.
Funny sounds like a bunny rabbit laughing
Funny feels like putting your hands on a bowl of wobbly jelly.

Josie Marshall (10)
Mill Hill School

Autumn Leaves

Autumn leaves
Under the trees,
Tumble, tumble, tumble down,
Up I climb, just in time,
My mam is shouting 'come here, now!'
Then she hears a mighty *ooow!*

Jessica Meldrum (9)
St Mary's RC Primary School, Sunderland

CONCENTRATION

C oncentration camps
O ver the hills the Germans fire
N early missing their air targets
C ause of fear
E ntering enemy barracks, fire at the enemy
N ever giving up firing to the end
T earing down forests and trees
R attling on the Jews' doors
A rtillery firing at each other
T ension mounting in the camps
I nto the depths of the dark
O ver the battered and torn trees
N *o mercy says Hitler.*

Camp

Michael Quinn (10)
St Mary's RC Primary School, Sunderland

WORLD WAR II

Guns shoot like rockets
People dying everywhere
Treeless and bleak battlefield
Scared and worried people wondering
If they will ever see their families again.
Bodies everywhere, dead families,
Heavy guns to be carried.

Jessica Scarlett (9)
St Mary's RC Primary School, Sunderland

A PARACHUTE VOYAGE
UP! UP! AND AWAY!

We're rising and rejoicing,
The whole world is beneath us.
We're flying, we're blowing,
With no noisy fuss.

Not the quickest way to travel,
Not the safest place to be,
But in truth, the whole wide world,
Under my feet I can see.

The scene is all so beautiful
The sky is clear and blue,
There is no sign of bad weather,
And the clouds are fluffy and new.

Now the weather gets so cold and bitter,
As the wind blows us south,
Causing me to shiver,
I'm so cold as a little mouse!

Then the wind blows us west,
And the clear blue sea foams into sight,
It twinkles, as if made of crystals,
When you are up at such a great height.

We are then tossed onto the north,
With snow tipped mountains found,
They glitter and shine with happiness,
But from them comes not a sound.

Then the warm wind blows us east,
The hot desert is now in sight,
We rest to enjoy the warmth for a while,
But we must move on, day is turning into night.

Lydia Samy (10)
St Mary's RC Primary School, Sunderland

THE VOYAGE

The ship left Southampton at quarter to two
The wind was harsh but the sea was blue
The waves frothed with unwanted spray,
and the sea air was bitterly cold.
The water barrel was almost dry,
and the food was covered with mould.
By the end of the month, the sailors were weak
and the future was looking bleak.
Very late the following night
the ship was pulled in by a curious light,
and underneath the silvery moon
was a lit up, deep, blue lagoon.
A beautiful girl with a sequinned tail lay poised in
                                    the golden sand.
The sailors gave a hearty cheer for they had reached
                                    the mermaid land.
And by the lagoon as the captain had said
was a turquoise whale from the seabed.

Alex Shanks (11)
St Mary's RC Primary School, Sunderland

MY JOURNEY THROUGH TIME

When I was small,
I used to crawl,
Onto my mum's lap.
She used to throw
Me up and down,
We joked around
And laughed.

But sadly now,
The past has gone,
And it's time
To move on.
No joking around,
No singing loud,
I must move on,
I'm older.

Hannah Watson (11)
St Mary's RC Primary School, Sunderland

BILL

Down the lane
Up the hill
Lives a man called Bill.
He's no ordinary man
Because he wears a frying pan
Attached to his belt
Which is made out of felt.
He has a dog called Billy
Who always sits on a lily
He's purple and blue
And aged two.

One day down the town
Bill had a frown
Found a girl named Jill.
They got married on a hill
Second day in marriage
Threw his wife in a carriage.
Crash, bash, boom
'I might eat my spoon'
Next day he couldn't eat his balloon.

Jenny Adshead (10)
St Mary's RC Primary School, Sunderland

STRANGER

Here he is,
this man of mystery.
There's a catastrophic mess all around me,
What do I say?
Do I say hello?
My heart says yes!
But my body says no.

I'm walking towards him,
I'm telling him my name,
But then all of a sudden,
My heart bursts like a flame.

The ocean behind me,
I turn around and see,
No one else is there,
Just a reflection of me,
Just a reflection of me.

Anna Maltby (10)
St Mary's RC Primary School, Sunderland

I AM A TIGER

I am a tiger hear my fight,
Look at me now day and night.
I am a tiger I can hunt out prey
Eat the meat with all my might.

I am a tiger scratching the log
Scratching more till it breaks with light.
Wait till I get free for life.

Connor Hall (7)
St Mary's RC Primary School, Sunderland

SCHOOL RULES

I love school very much
although we don't have a rabbit in a hutch.
We have lots of school rules
like football is banned on the field.
We have to work very hard
my favourite lesson is maths.
At Beads World I learned to thatch
I have lots of friends.
When the school year ends
My friends jump about like hens.
But I just, just say I miss school rules.
Sometimes I am so upset I drool.

Alice Wilson (9)
St Mary's RC Primary School, Sunderland

HEARD IT IN THE PLAYGROUND

I play alone
In the playground
No one to play with
In the playground.
Left alone
In the playground.
Tears fall down my face
In the playground.
It's unfair
In the playground.

Liam Gillespie (7)
St Mary's RC Primary School, Sunderland

SKY'S BAD DAY!

My dog Sky went to the vet
Sky is my best pet.
She never bites in all her life
'Oh dear' it is Sky's bad day.

She bit the vet on his bum,
Oh what glorious fun she had.
She chased him round and round
and his glass fell on the ground.

The dog pills fell, the dog flew
out into the reception room.
She knocks the Coca Cola machine and
it went boom.
'Oh dear' it is Sky's bad day.

Hannah Mitchinson (8)
St Mary's RC Primary School, Sunderland

MEALTIME FOR SHARKS

The swift and silent shark
glides through the crystal blue water
with its back baking in the sun.

Within the dark cold depths of the water,
The shark darts through the jagged coral
looking for its prey.

With teeth as sharp as steel
it grips on to its prey
and swallows it whole.

Ben Herring (8)
St Mary's RC Primary School, Sunderland

THE CRUISE

On a cruise I touched a fuse,
everyone saw the light shining in the night,
after I fell over,
I got pushed in the limo by a gofer,
I thought I must have been dreaming,
until I saw the gofer gleaming,
he asked me where I wanted to go,
I replied 'I don't know.'
He pushed me out on my own,
in the dark all alone.

I got a taxi to the cruise,
They said 'Ha ha, you lose.'
They punched my stomach,
and stole my one hundre-year-old comic.
That was when I got tossed out,
I began to shout,
'A car just ran me over,'
then a van pulled over,
and took me to Dover,
then his van turned to a rover.

He dropped me off at the cruise,
but it wasn't working because of the fuse,
then I saw a line of queues,
to get off the boat,
but they fell in the moat.
I decided to go back home,
and had a biscuit with my gnome.

Lewis Monte (10)
St Mary's RC Primary School, Sunderland

THE CHEEKY GREMLIN

Behind the washing machine in my house
You will find something green.
He is not one of my sister's toys,
He is a gremlin who's never seen.

Once before I think I've seen him,
He has brown eyes, and a cheeky grin.
Sometimes my sister sees him
Scavenging in the bin.

I tried to take a photograph
He just ran and hid
I tried to find him
It just made him more scared.
I wanted just one photograph
To take and show my class.

Martha Craggs (9)
St Mary's RC Primary School, Sunderland

SOLAR SYSTEM

Planets, planets everywhere
The moon, the stars and Jupiter.
And lots of other planets too.
We saw the eclipse of the moon
It was very exciting too.

Mars, Venus are the best
All the rest are in such a mess.

Anna White (10)
St Mary's RC Primary School, Sunderland

GO-KARTS

Speeding, speeding down the track
in black round bends with friends
over humps jumping bumps
fleeing faster getting past more
skidding, spinning round the bends
getting slower is the motor
driving in stop in a min.

Refuelled round again
skipping bends changing gears
cold ears fearing crashes
dashing, bashing, thrashing,
smashing.
Came first with a burst
smashed up.
Win the cup.

Jack Bengochea (10)
St Mary's RC Primary School, Sunderland

THE DEATH OF A NINJA

My face burns with torch fire.
My skilful opponent is looking down at me.
His samurai sword is through me.
He killed me with stealth and honour.
My hair is a mess, that's tangled up.
My clothes are stained with blood.
But now my soul and heart are clear.

Adam McDade (11)
St Mary's RC Primary School, Sunderland

Up And Down The Lonely Forest

As I wander up and down,
I shiver with a fearful feeling,
Of something jumping out,
Of the big, never-ending forest.

I hear the lonely cries of the forest trees,
I stumble over a rock,
As it moves, I run,
Not daring to stop for a breath.

I see a house,
I run in to find,
A great hungry bear,
Something behind and something in front.

I go out to find,
Not a single sound,
Not a bird chirping,
Nor a rustle of the leaves.

I run to the cliff edge,
And a great, huge shout,
A flutter of wings,
And another great, huge roar.

Something begins to climb,
As I begin to run,
The rustle of leaves has a loud echo,
And the birds flutter and chirp, once again.

I run across to the other edge of the cliff,
Another shout,
I run to the forest, the only safe place,
Until I realise the mistake I made.

But I run to the other end of the forest,
The shouting close behind,
To the light I run,
To find the other edge of the cliff.

No place to go,
Should I give in? I cannot decide,
The shouting drawing closer,
They come and get me.

Alice Haley (10)
St Mary's RC Primary School, Sunderland

THE STAFFROOM

I walked outside the staffroom,
The time was ten to nine.
Some throw paper aeroplanes,
With spare homework from F9.
Others start to gamble,
While my teacher starts a fight.
He punches the caretaker as he stumbles,
What a sight.
'Yes' he shouted with glory,
'Down in the first round.'
Then came the next contender,
Mr Barker the angry head.
He smacked him in the belly,
And nearly knocked him dead.
I ran into the courtyard,
To tell all my friends.
As the teachers came out,
The fun unfortunately had to end.

Joseph Collins (10)
St Mary's RC Primary School, Sunderland

THE MONSTER'S CAVE

There were spikes as big as dinosaur teeth
Slime like leaking treacle
Sticking to your feet
And cobwebs
With only bone left
Of spiders.

Drips of blood
Coming from the ceiling.
A sour smell.
It smelt like smelly socks.
Sweet blood tastes come from
the ceiling making a pound
                    on the floor.

Zara Taylor (8)
St Mary's RC Primary School, Sunderland

BUTTERFLY

B   eautiful colours on a butterfly's wings
U   nder and over flowers so beautiful
T   rees and flowers are what they love best
T   ell me how they fly so prettily.
E   scaping from the cocoon
R   evealing all of its colour
F   lying far into the sky
L   ilies and sunflowers they land on and lots more flowers
Y   ou see them fluttering in the sky on a bright summer's day.

Leanne Hutcheon (9)
St Mary's RC Primary School, Sunderland

MY HANDS

My hands are helpful like a friend
My hands are like hot fire
My hands are dirty like muck
I'm glad I've got my hands
My hands can dance to music
My hands can clap to a song
My hands can communicate
My hands can wave like a friendly smile
My hands can wipe my eyes when I cry
I'm glad I've got hands
My hands are like butterflies prancing in the
                                         fresh breeze
My hands are like petals on a flower
My hands are like a mum
I'm glad I've got my hands.

Claudia Anderson (7)
St Mary's RC Primary School, Sunderland

MY DOG JESS

My dog Jess is a very funny dog
She jumps around the house all day
Even in the fog!
You know it is very funny
The way she jumps around,
She goes around in circles,
While sitting on the ground!

Sarah Anderson (9)
St Mary's RC Primary School, Sunderland

MY DREAM GOAL!

Everybody in their seats,
Match about to start,
Sunderland win the kick-off,
Kev and Niall to start,
Pass back to Mickey Gray,
Then on the wing to Arca,
Pass it on to Hutchsion,
And then a pass to Kevin,
He'll do some skill past defenders,
Then a cross for Quinn,
He rises high and headers it in,
And that was my 'dream goal'.

Jonathan Meldrum (10)
St Mary's RC Primary School, Sunderland

OTTERS PLAYING IN THE POOL

Now you see me
Now you don't
Then you'll spot me
Then you won't.
I am an otter just having a play
And I can swim in any different way.
Bobbing and bouncing out of the water,
Looking for fish is a hungry otter.
So say 'hooray' that we otters are alive
And always wish that we will survive.

Clare Dewhurst (9)
St Mary's RC Primary School, Sunderland

AIR ATTACK

Taxi to runway
Line up on the line
Wait of the controller
And at the time
Release the brakes
Apply full power
Pull back the stick
And we're air borne.

Higher, higher
Make a sharp right turn
Towards the danger zone
Down to one hundred feet
You will see a marker cone
Now shoot the missile
At the enemy fleet
Now return to base
Before the Iraqis find out
Gear down, reduce speed
To one hundred mph 100 ft . . . 50ft . . . 20ft . . .
And hit the ground with power.

Jonathan Rasmussen (11)
St Mary's RC Primary School, Sunderland

HAPPY THINGS

When things are happy, I am happy.
When things are happy, God likes you.
When things are happy, I think of Jesus.
When things are happy, I like you.

Jimmy Kordbarlag (9)
St Mary's RC Primary School, Sunderland

A Journey Through Knowledge

As the fire orange masts
On a ship of pale blue
Sail through oceans of flowing additions.

As the thick entwining branches
With paper-thin green leaves
Climb up broad poles of s-p-e-l-l-i-n-g-s

As the thin sailor men
Fall from their boats into raging tides
Of ancient history times.

As the jet black spider
Spins some more
Of his intellectual World Wide Web.

Gabrielle O'Connor (10)
St Mary's RC Primary School, Sunderland

World War II

I was running only to hear cries for help.
I was covered in red rain which came from enemies
who died alone or together.
Long here is just the same, bang, boom, dead.
I fell down a bank to where I landed.
I hid in the soft bloody grass where I was found by a German.
I ran behind a blown-up bomb where I took my rifle and shot.
There were a few moments of bravery in me and that was it.

Daniel Dale (9)
St Mary's RC Primary School, Sunderland

THE GOLDEN EAGLE

Golden wings, a cream white head,
Its soothing cry, could revive the dead,
Circling mountains, searching for prey,
This huge, magnificent bird!

Shroo . . . Shroo . . . Shroo . . . Ka!

A beautiful creature, which God created,
To live a life, of excitement and adventure.
It loves to fly, swoop and dive,
This huge, magnificent bird!

Shroo . . . Shroo . . . Shroo . . . Ka!

The Golden Eagle, King of them all,
Could die out, sure to fall,
Being taken away, from its loving world,
This huge, magnificent bird!

Shroo . . . Shroo . . . Kaa!

John-Paul Cosgrove (11)
St Mary's RC Primary School, Sunderland

SUMMER

The azure sky holds a golden ball,
That shimmers on the lush green grass.
Twittering birds glide under the swaying
                    branches of a big brown tree.
Radiant flowers stand proudly
Near the glinting water's edge.

Jennifer Brown (8)
St Mary's RC Primary School, Sunderland

SPLASH

Splash, splash, splash, said the heavy, thrashing rain,
Splash, splash, splash, said the rain, again.
The rain was swishing round and round,
Then another raindrop splashed straight on the ground.

Another raindrop splashed straight at my coat,
Then one more went shooting down my throat.
One more raindrop splashed at my toes,
Then another splashed on the tip of my nose.

Millions fell down,
All over the town.
I looked straight up at the sky
Then another raindrop splashed straight in my eye.

Michael Simpson (9)
St Mary's RC Primary School, Sunderland

ALIENS

One scary night I had a frightful dream.
An alien from outer space looking very mean.
I stared at him, he stared at me, I got a shock.
The alien from outer space was wearing a Roman frock.
He held a gun black, blue and red
Suddenly I tumbled out of bed.
The next night I had another dream
The aliens came again
But this time with eighteen.

James Beaton (10)
St Mary's RC Primary School, Sunderland

A DAY TO REGRET!

See the big cruise liner about to depart
From the lonely deck
Where it was to all start.

Sailing through the Antarctic ocean
The white horses are waves
Charging with great motion.

The captain sounds the horn so
Near it can't be heard and impossible to hear.

Quick turn the ship everyone heard for in the distance
Was an iceberg.

Everyone quick, lifebelts on
The ship is sinking and soon will be gone.

The ship disappeared
Everyone dead
They sunk and sunk to their ice beds.

People in boats had ice cold breath
Cold and miserable
Close to death.

The spirit of death hung over the sea, but nobody
Knew this was meant to be.

Victoria Barlow (11)
St Mary's RC Primary School, Sunderland

ROLLER COASTER

Spinning round and round
Up and down faster
Upside down screaming
Shouting spinning
Screaming shouting
Faster, faster need to
Go faster, slowing
Down even more
Suddenly stopped.

Nearly fell out
Again, again I
Shouted more,
More I screamed
I wanted more
Fun, fast, mint,
Great so fast
Tearing my head
Off.

Feel sick, feel sick
No more, no more
Please, please no more
Need to get off, need to get off
Getting faster and faster
Stop, stop, stop the ride
Help, help get me off
Need help loads and
Loads of *help!*

Victoria Campbell (10)
St Mary's RC Primary School, Sunderland

THE DULL SEAGULL

The seagull felt dull,
So he flew south then west,
And fell on a man's chest,
Then he flew north
And then east
And fought a wildebeest,
Then he flew home,
Ate an ice cream cone,
But the gull still felt dull.

So he went to visit a bear
But he said 'Honestly I don't care'
So he went to visit the bee
But he hid in a tree
He went in to visit the pig
But he chewed on a twig,
But the gull still felt dull.

So he stayed at home and had a drone,
In front of the TV.
While he thought why me?
For he tried a fish,
To put on his dish,
But he simply just missed.

But the gull was still dull.

Megan Campbell (10)
St Mary's RC Primary School, Sunderland

SATURDAY NIGHT

Every single Saturday night,
I phone up my friends, they're such a sight.
Lauren, Rebecca, Bethany too,
And of course all the rest of the crew.

So the arrangements were finished and made
We were to meet down the arcade.
I washed my face, got out my clothes
Did up my hair and powdered my nose.

I got out all my bits and bobs
Put on my high heels that sound like clogs
I phoned a taxi ring, ring, ring
We were down the town ready to sing.

Hannah Matterson (10)
St Mary's RC Primary School, Sunderland

MONGREL

M y dog is a mongrel.
O n the night she is a pest.
N ot on the morning she is too tired.
G rowling, not a chance.
R eally nice dogs are mongrels.
E ven if she is kicked she doesn't growl.
L ovely dog she is.

Meghan Turnbull (10)
St Mary's RC Primary School, Sunderland

MONSTER

Her home, she calls it darkened from the world.
Lies in the mist, the mist swirled.
It is very easy to see.
But very hard to find.

Victims screaming then . . . silent.
Heroes go but don't come back.
They don't expect to find
In their wildest dreams and mind.

Her hair, well not hair at all.
All her victims fastly fall.
Her hair withering, slithering, screeching,
Snakes her hair poisonous green.
Always heard but never seen.

Grey her face
Evil her look.
Killing down the human race.
Even her snakes looking sly.

Listen now and listen well.
For I am going to tell.
What she is and what she isn't.
Medusa is her name.
And killing is her game.

Bethany Patience (10)
St Mary's RC Primary School, Sunderland

FEELINGS

Happiness is my mam
Unhappiness is when somebody dies
Joy is seeing my dad
Sadness is when Molly is ill
Anger is another cat hurting Muffin
Fear is the dentist
Butterflies was when I nearly fell out the roller coaster
Gladness is going home after school
Excitement is roller coasters
Terror is when I have nightmares
Hate is living away from Dad
Love is my family
Envy is Abbie having fish and not me.

Hannah Jervis (7)
St Mary's RC Primary School, Sunderland

SNOWFALL

S nowfall is a joyful thought
N either rain, sun, it cannot be bought
O h I wish I could be a dollop of snow
W eather never seems to grow.
F luttering down
A ll earth makes no sound
L aying waiting to be found
L ightly flowing to the ground.

Samantha Yewdell (10)
St Mary's RC Primary School, Sunderland

THE FROZEN STREET

People in the window laughing at a man,
Half frozen on the street dead as a doorman.
As the snow falls on the man half dead,
People are now staring at a big deathbed.
And as he floats up to the heavens high,
They gasp in horror as they say goodbye.
Now or never they should answer the door,
To the man who has lost his soul and more.
But they will not dare to open the latch on the
big fat door, to the cold outside world where
                                    nature rules all.

Josh Parkinson (10)
St Mary's RC Primary School, Sunderland

THE OLYMPICS

The Olympics starts every four years with events
such as the sprint and hurdles and lots more.
With women and men battling for the gold
from different countries such as the USA.
The javelin is thrown as long as a football pitch
along with the shot put.
The freestyle splashes along with the torches ashes,
and divers jump when the boxers bump
and the sprinting never ends.
The marathon goes on for miles who will get to the end?
The high jump goes right up high along with the pole vault.
I wonder who will win this year, I wonder.

Michael Knox (10)
St Mary's RC Primary School, Sunderland

TWENTY-FOUR HOURS ON THE BEACH

Hear the waves crashing to the shore
see the glorious golden sand
and hear a distant roar.

Hear the children running
out of the sea to the ice cream van
little ones shouting
get one for me.

As the day is fading
and the night draws near
there was only a silent sound
you could possibly hear.

Now the night has arrived
and brought with it the stars
now you can't hear the sea roar
you only hear the cars.

It is morn again thank God for that
and everyone is here
and all the children are playing again
because night will soon be near.

Alexandra Cain (11)
St Mary's RC Primary School, Sunderland

WHEN I GOT MY HAMSTER

When I got my hamster
She was only four weeks old
She was taken away from
Her brothers and sisters
When she was only four weeks old.

When I got my hamster
She was scared and I couldn't pick her up
But now she's big old and fat
I love her very much.

Natalie Stidolph (11)
Stanhope County Primary School

THE STORM

A storm is raging through the town,
The wind wrestles rain to the ground.
A thunderbolt pierces the charcoal sky,
The frail old sun fades and dies.

The wind howls through lanes and streets,
This is how Satan goes to preach.
You quiver as you hear the thunder,
Mother Nature has caused a blunder.

The sacred sun battles the worthy opponent,
The globe of fire is triumphant over his mighty component.
The wind becomes a breeze of placid peace,
The rain is rare and droplets cease.

There are blue skies all around,
White clouds are far and few,
The earth is fresh, colourful and new.
The world is filled with the birds song.
Once again the storm has gone.

Louise Young (11)
Stanhope County Primary School

MY GUINEA PIGS ARE LOTS OF FUN

My guinea pigs are lots of fun,
I like to let them out to run,
They like to eat the grass and clover,
Then I give them a brush all over.

They eat different foods,
They are such cool dudes,
Jumpy is tan and Blossom is white,
They both give you a fright in the night!

When you try to touch them,
They sometimes scratch your hand,
But they don't mean to frighten you,
So try and understand.

Ashleigh Keenan (9)
Stanhope County Primary School

PETS

Pets can be gruesome
Pets can be nice
Cats, dogs, hamsters and mice.
Pets can be funny
Pets can be boring.
I can still hear the lion from the zoo roaring.
Pets can be young
Pets can be old
Some pets can even do as they're told.

Kassie Waugh (11)
Stanhope County Primary School

In The Woods

Once I had a stroll in the woods,
And I've never known it be such a wonderful sight.
It gave you a warm and happy feeling,
As you walk under the shade of the trees,
That black out the sun's light.

The delicate rosebuds rise in the summer breeze,
As the ivy cling to the trunks of the trees.
I stop and listen to the small animal calls,
And the rushing water in the distance, from a waterfall.

The dew trickles off weeds and leaves,
As small colourful birds fly from tree to tree.
Now the sun is setting, making pretty colours in the sky,
And as I walk home, I turn round to the woods and
whisper goodbye.

Victoria Liscombe (10)
Stanhope County Primary School

Space Aliens From Mars

Space aliens from maybe Mars
I don't know where they come from
Maybe from the stars
They come down in a UFO
When they come I don't know
I'm scared and I shiver and shiver
This time the space aliens
Get bigger and bigger.

Emmy Simpson (9)
Stanhope County Primary School

THE BIG BANG

Bang! The universe expands like a bird expanding his wings.
On it goes, on and on until a quarter way through
Then another bang, it's getting faster, it's at light speed now.
It's formed a few galaxies and now it's half way through
Colouring in the white sheets of paper, racing like a hound
                                        chasing a fox.
Carrying out his master's orders, catch that fox, catch that fox!
It's almost there and bang, it's done!
Its dust forms the planets and the heat forms the stars,
This is how time began.

James McElwee (11)
Stanhope County Primary School

ENTRAPMENT MOUNTAIN

It seemed a challenge
To test it to the max
Give me to think.

The danger lurks in front
But I'll be ready
I grip my arm tighter.

I get to the top
King of the world
See the world spread below.

Stop . . .
Avalanche
I awake entrampment.

Jonathan Wilson (11)
Stanhope County Primary School

THE HORRIBLE SATS

I am thinking of the horrible SATs
Wondering if I will pass
Will I get a high score
To get a Level five or a Level four.

When the paper gets put on my desk
Then comes the real test.
Will it be English, science or the maths?
Still wondering if I will pass.

Sitting nervous in my chair
Wondering if everyone will do the test fair.
Oh no look the test is maths
Still wondering if I will pass.

Now the SATs are over
And I can now relax.
No more of the horrible SATs
And guess what? I passed!

Paul Nygaard (11)
Stanhope County Primary School

THE BAD-TEMPERED SEA

The bad-tempered sea
Was vandalising the rocks
The cliff glanced at the sea
With its fierce grey eyes
Then threw itself into the sea.

Anthony Hall (11)
Stanhope County Primary School

PLAYTIMES

I hate playtimes
Bullies pushing you about
People standing around
Not even playing.

I hate playtimes
Get hit kids cry
People playing stupid games
Not fair.

I hate playtimes
Teachers yelling at kids
People fighting and arguing
Go away.

Lyndsey McGowell (11)
Stanhope County Primary School

BOOKS

Books are so colourful and bright
They are such a beautiful sight
Lots of funny poems to read
Lots of stories with a brilliant lead.

Lots of interesting words in a book
You can't resist to have a look
Different books have different scenes
With love stories, horror stories and magic dreams.

Kayleigh Kirkley (11)
Stanhope County Primary School

SCHOOL

Morning rises, back to school again,
Into the gates and into school.
Work begins, playtime comes.
Kids bomb dive in corners playing hopscotch again.
Bell rings, kids stop their games and into the line again.
Up the stairs, kids push their way into the classroom
and into their chairs.

Lauren Caizley (9)
Stanhope County Primary School

THE LONELY SCARECROW

All alone I stand in the field feeling lonely and sad,
My only visitors come and go without a sound.
They hover above in the sky all around,
They dare not come near, because I fill them with fear.
I stand alone and shed a small tear.

Dean Bill (10)
Stanhope County Primary School

FLY FLY FLY AWAY

Up in the air the other day
I saw a kite fly away
It flew, flew all the way
Till it stopped yesterday.
    Fly fly fly away.

Melissa Liddle (9)
Stanhope County Primary School

GRANDAD

I liked it when I heard him laugh
But I can't now,
It happened when I was four
But I'm not now.
Mum says I shouldn't look back
But I do.
She knows I love him,
She does.
I didn't go to the funeral
I didn't.
I wouldn't want to either,
I know he's gone,
But the pain hasn't.

Robyn Hamilton (9)
Stanhope County Primary School

RAINDROPS

R   eady or not here it comes
A   big black cloud
I   n the sky all around
N   ot a sound.

D   own goes the sun
R   ound the wind blows
O   n the count of one, two, three
P   op goes the raincloud
S   o now it is over me.

Michael Lister (9)
Stanhope County Primary School

THE NASTY TREE

The tree grabbed me, rattled me around,
Picked me up and slammed me on the ground.
It slapped me right in the face,
Tied me up in my disgrace.
It tripped me up and played with me,
Oooooo! What a tree!

Leonard Oxley (11)
Stanhope County Primary School

WHAT AM I?

A greedy pig
A hole digger
A squeaky mess
A fat lump
A carrot chewer
A lettuce eater.

I live in a cage, what am I?

Lee Alderson (10)
Stanhope County Primary School

RED

Red is a fire engine zooming by,
Red is a heart and the eyes of a fly.
Red is a top on the glue,
Or maybe a juicy apple too.
What's your favourite colour, mine is blue!

Lewis McHaffie (10)
Stanhope County Primary School

IN THE WOOD

In the wood there are trees
Through the trees there's a path
Down by the path there's a stream
Over top of the steam is a bridge
Across the bridge there are bluebells
By the bluebells snuffles a hedgehog
Beside the hedgehog there's a green leaf
On the green leave is a caterpillar
Next to the caterpillar is a ring
On the ring is a stone
In the stone is a magical world waiting
Waiting to welcome you in.

Victoria Naisby (11)
Stanhope County Primary School

ANIMALS

I like animals,
I like them big and small
I like fluffy ones,
In fact I like them all.

I like the ones that fly,
And I like the ones that jump really high.
I like the ones that swim in the sea,
I even like the bumblebee.

I like animals short and tall,
In fact as I've already said,
I like them all.

Rachel Codling (9)
Stanhope County Primary School

THE NASTY WIND

Today I went outside and got a fright
The wind tried to blow me out of sight
We struggled and tugged
But I lost and the wind blew me down
With a powerful thrust.

It threw me down and pushed me around
It punched me high with a horrible sound.
It swallowed me up and spat me out
I felt as if I'd had a good clout.

So when you see the wind about
Just stop in, don't go out.
It's a menace I can say
The danger is it will blow you away.

Michael Smith (10)
Stanhope County Primary School

VOLCANO AND MY DAD

My dad went to a volcano
He thought it was going to blow
But my oh my how wrong could he be
Because it started to snow.

He ran down the mountain
With a hop skip jump
But he tripped over some lava
And landed with a bump.

Jessica Lee (10)
Stanhope County Primary School

THE WITCH'S POTION

Some snake to uncoil.
The muddy soil.
Some curdling phlegm.
Then count to ten.
Some sewer water.
To chew your daughter.
Some blood curdling venom.
To send you to heaven.

Some dead man's things
To mingle with lungs.
Some sharp, black nails
With puppy dog tails.
With centipedes
No good deeds.
So make this bubble
We need some trouble.

Andrea Gilmour (11)
Stanhope County Primary School

THE NASTY WIND

The nasty wind spins around,
Standing thirty foot off the ground,
Making a whistling sound.

It goes around destroying towns,
And all the people run and frown,
Whilst leaving town.

Liam Fraser (10)
Stanhope County Primary School

In The Future Sea

In the future sea,
Will people live there like you and me?
Will the seaweed catch the fish?
Will the sharks get their favourite dish?
Will the fish begin to talk?
Will the eels begin to walk?
Will we not see the city?
Will it be under the sea?
Waiting to be risen by you and me?
Will the animals be extinct?
Will they not even think?
Will boats conk out?
Will icebergs be allowed out?
Some animals have disappeared,
But some animals have just appeared.

Adam Ratcliffe (11)
Stanhope County Primary School

My Kenning - David Beckham

Free-kick taker
Money maker
Good scorer
Ball giver
Hair carer
Photo poser
Autograph signer
Vic lover
Brooklyn father.

Jack Wright (10)
Witherwack Primary School

MY KENNING - THE BIG SHOW

Advert maker
The rock hater
Money giver
Seven footer
Five hundred pounder
Ring splatter
Opponent climber
Consistent winner
Shane's partner
McChman follower
Intimidating wrestler
Wife lover
Mother hugger
Car pusher.

Charlotte Nash (11)
Witherwack Primary School

MY KENNING - MATTHEW MY BROTHER

Brother annoyer
Loud winger
Power Ranger watcher
Constant Smiler
Mum lover
Sister follower
Pokémon card collector.

Lee Jennings (10)
Witherwack Primary School

MY KENNING - MY BROTHER

Tear crier
Good sleeper
Video watcher
Cuddle giver
Pop singer
Shaky dancer
Dinner pincher
Yoghurt eater
Love bringer.

Toni Peel (11)
Witherwack Primary School

MY KENNING - DAD

Heavy sleeper
Football player
TV watcher
Brilliant worker
Loud sneezer
Baby feeder
Silence breaker
Snore maker.

Kim Scott (10)
Witherwack Primary School

MY KENNING - RONALDO

Left striker
Speedy runner
Magazine poser
Money maker
Corner taker
Goal scorer
Brazil's player.

Christopher Dawkins (10)
Witherwack Primary School

MY KENNING - TIGER

A child killer
A bone cruncher
A fast runner
A good hider
A head sucker
A human chaser
A deer eater
A man murderer.

Ryan Newton (11)
Witherwack Primary School

MY KENNING - HAMSTER

Supersleeper
Never sees ya!
Ball lover
Fast runner
Treat grabber.

Craig Ord (10)
Witherwack Primary School

MY KENNING - ME

Chocolate lover
Vegetable hater
Friday night swinger
Story reader
Big dreamer
Not a friend taker
Accident maker
Computer player
Super sleeper
Ice cream eater
Friend maker
Big brother
Big lover
Art creator
Message forgetter.

Kurt Ramsay (11)
Witherwack Primary School

MY KENNING - CROCODILE

Meat lover
Bone cruncher
Jaw snapper
Scale peeler
River swimmer
Sun basker.

Sophie Byers (11)
Witherwack Primary School

MY KENNING - MY TEACHER

Hard worker
Homework giver
Lesson planner
Book marker
Constant sneezer
Wine drinker
Dinner burner
Food eater
Specs wearer
Snappy dresser
Morning swimmer
Children lover.

Christopher Smith (10)
Witherwack Primary School

MY KENNING - LION

Food cruncher
Meat eater
Fast runner
Good hunter
Sneaky pouncer
Excellent camouflager
Fierce skinner
Deer muncher
Good senser.

Jordan Taylor (10)
Witherwack Primary School

MY KENNING - MY MAM

Money giver
Present buyer
Coffee drinker,
Dinner maker,
Hard worker,
Cuddle receiver,
Child carer,
Home helper,
Music listener.

Louise Carr (11)
Witherwack Primary School

MY KENNING - MY AUNT

Money giver
Tea drinker
Funny joker
Soap washer
Caring lover
Help giver
Bingo player
Shopping hater
Embarrassment maker.

Raymond McCririe (10)
Witherwack Primary School